Grammar Matters
Teaching Grammar in Adult ESL Programs

K. Lynn Savage
with
Gretchen Bitterlin
and Donna Price

CAMBRIDGE UNIVERSITY PRESS
Cambridge, New York, Melbourne, Madrid, Cape Town, Singapore,
São Paulo, Delhi, Dubai, Tokyo

Cambridge University Press
32 Avenue of the Americas, New York, NY 10013-2473, USA

www.cambridge.org

© Cambridge University Press 2010

This publication is in copyright. Subject to statutory exception
and to the provisions of relevant collective licensing agreements,
no reproduction of any part may take place without the written
permission of Cambridge University Press.

First published 2010

Printed in the United States of America

ISBN-13 978-1-107-90730-0 paperback

Table of Contents

Introduction   1

1   The Role of Grammar in Adult ESL   2

2   An Eclectic Approach to Teaching Grammar   5

3   Choosing Grammar to Teach   11

4   The Grammar Lesson: Presentation   16

5   The Grammar Lesson: Guided Practice   22

6   The Grammar Lesson: Communicative Practice   31

Conclusion   38

References   40

Introduction

ESL students in adult education classes are very diverse in age, educational background, and employment history. They may be as young as 16 or as old as 90. Some may have had no education in their countries of origin and be unable to read or write in their first language; others may have multiple college degrees and speak several languages. Some are young adults who have never worked; others may have had professional positions in their native countries. These students also have diverse goals: to survive in a new culture, to find a job, to help their children with their homework, to obtain additional education for themselves.

The one characteristic that all these students have in common is the need and desire to learn English. However, even in this area they have very diverse experiences, especially related to the learning of English grammar. Here are examples of two students from the same class.

> Chao Yang had almost no formal education in his country, Laos; in fact, he has never studied his native Hmong language in written form. In the United States he has picked up basic conversational English at his job, but his writing skills are very weak. All grammar terminology is foreign to him.

> Sonia Rachinsky is a nuclear scientist from Russia who studied English in her own country with the grammar-translation method. She has a good understanding of the verb tenses and loves grammar exercises, but she has trouble expressing herself in everyday conversation. She doesn't feel she is learning English unless the teacher explains the rules of grammar.

The goal of this booklet is to help teachers develop and deliver grammar lessons that are effective and relevant with a range of students: those with as little grammar background as Chao's or as much as Sonia's, as well as all those students who fall somewhere between these two extremes.

The first three chapters explore the role of grammar in adult ESL and propose an eclectic approach to teaching grammar that encompasses selected elements from a variety of earlier approaches to language teaching. We look at factors that determine the grammar our adult learners need and at characteristics of language that affect the selection of grammar to teach. Chapters 4 to 6 describe three stages of a grammar lesson, with an emphasis on oral communication: presentation, guided practice, and communicative practice. In addition to defining the purpose of each stage and the teacher's role, these chapters offer a sample of activities appropriate to the respective stages.

1 | *The Role of Grammar in Adult ESL*

Most practitioners in the field of adult ESL agree that it is important to teach grammar. But what is grammar? Do we all mean the same thing when we use this word?

The answer, of course, is no. At different times during the long history of second-language instruction, grammar has been regarded as a set of rules ("third person singular present-tense verbs take an *-s* for subject-verb agreement"; "adjectives go before nouns") to be memorized. Today, grammar is still taught and tested this way in many parts of the world.

The problem with this knowledge-transmission approach to grammar is that for most students it leads to limited language acquisition. Most of us are familiar with the phenomenon of students who know the rules of grammar but who are nonetheless unable to ask for simple directions. As a result of this observed gap between knowledge of grammar and its successful application, there has been a shift in our view of grammar instruction over the last 20 or 30 years. Nowadays, many ESL practitioners view grammar less as a body of knowledge to be studied than as a skill to be practiced and developed. Grammar knowledge is important, but only insofar as it enables students to communicate "accurately, meaningfully, and appropriately" (Larsen-Freeman, 2001).

This chapter supports the view of grammar as a skill to be taught and examines three roles that underlie the importance of grammar in adult ESL education:

- Grammar as an enabling skill
- Grammar as a motivator
- Grammar as a means to self-sufficiency

Grammar as an enabling skill

Though a skill in its own right, grammar can also be regarded as a necessary "master" skill that enables competence to develop in the areas of listening, speaking, reading, and writing. When grammar is incorrect or misunderstood in any of these areas, communication may be disrupted, as the following examples illustrate.

Listening. Imagine a teacher who says, "Please bring me the books," only to have a student bring her just one book because the student did not hear the plural *-s* or understand what it means. In this case, a better understanding of the underlying grammar would have improved the student's listening ability.

Speaking. In a job interview, an applicant is asked, "How long have you been working at your current job?" The applicant replies, "I worked there for two years." The interviewer wonders: Is the applicant still working there or not? In this situation, knowledge of the present perfect would have enabled the student to reply more accurately.

Reading. Trying to follow the directions for assembling a bookcase, a student reads *Slide the bookcase close to the wall after tightening all of the pieces.* Not knowing that *after* signals the first of the two actions in the sentence, the student performs the actions in reverse order.

Writing. Filling out a form at his job in an automotive repair shop, an automotive tech student writes *I check the brakes.* Reading the report, the supervisor is confused: Did the student already check the brakes? Is he going to check the brakes? If the student had written *checked* on the report, there would have been no ambiguity.

These examples illustrate the role of grammar as the foundation upon which all the other skills are built. Efficient communication cannot take place without correct grammar.

Grammar as a motivator

Many ESL students firmly believe that knowledge of grammar is essential to their being able to acquire a new language. These are the students who, when responding to a needs assessment, typically say, "I want to study grammar. If I know grammar very well, I'll be able to speak well and get a good job." Students who have studied English in their own countries often equate language learning with learning grammar. Students who have acquired English imperfectly in this country through interactions with native speakers also recognize the importance of grammar, as they may have encountered misunderstandings because of their grammar errors. When adult ESL courses include a strong grammar component in the curriculum, both of these groups of students may be more motivated to attend or return to school.

Just as many students are motivated to learn grammar, many teachers are strongly motivated to teach it. When our students express a desire to learn grammar, most teachers naturally respond by trying to provide what students want. Moreover, most adult schools have a mandated course syllabus, which is frequently a grammar syllabus or a whole-language syllabus with an addendum listing grammatical structures to teach. Such a tool is an impetus for us to provide grammar instruction. A third motivating factor is our background as teachers: Many of us, having learned foreign languages via grammar-based methodologies or as a consequence of our teacher training and education, are more comfortable teaching grammar than other language skills.

Grammar as a means to self-sufficiency

Most ESL students expect teachers to correct their grammar errors, but a more practical goal is for students to learn to correct their own mistakes. Grammar instruction assists English learners in becoming aware of a structure and then continuing to notice it in subsequent encounters (Fotos, 2001). Once students have internalized the structure through repeated exposure, they can use this knowledge to monitor their own language use.

The ability to self-correct is particularly desirable for students with job-related or educational goals. At work, students are often required to write notes, e-mail messages, and reports, so they need to be able to communicate accurately in writing. If students haven't learned how to monitor themselves, they could have problems with such tasks. An understanding of grammar is also important for ESL learners who plan to transition to vocational programs or college. These students need to understand the meaning of grammatical structures as they listen to lectures and read manuals and textbooks, as well as to use the forms correctly when they make oral presentations and write papers.

The ability to self-correct leads to self-sufficiency. Regardless of their proficiency level or goals, almost all students can benefit from learning English grammar.

2 An Eclectic Approach to Teaching Grammar

Historically, language-teaching methods have alternated between two opposing approaches: those that focus on analyzing the language and those that focus on using it. At one end of the spectrum, students learn about the grammar, sounds, and vocabulary of the language, but they may seldom or never be required to use it in meaningful communication. At the other end, students begin using the language immediately in order to acquire it (Larsen-Freeman, 2001). To this day, we can find these contrasting positions reflected in adult ESL courses in the United States. Some teachers and programs approach language teaching from a grammar-oriented perspective while others favor a more communicative approach.

These days, however, more and more practitioners realize that the two orientations – grammar-based and communicative – have elements that complement each other and that, when combined, can result in an eclectic approach that is effective in teaching grammar to adult students. The purpose of this chapter is to identify those elements and to describe how each can contribute to effective grammar teaching. The chapter covers the following topics:

- The place of grammar in earlier language-teaching approaches and methods
- Competency-based education (CBE)
- Larsen-Freeman's three-dimensional grammar model
- Features of an eclectic approach to grammar instruction

The place of grammar in earlier approaches and methods

Many earlier language-teaching methods included elements that can be effective in teaching grammar to adult ESL students, yet the methods in their "pure" versions have been found to be inadequate in addressing these students' needs. The advantages as well as the limitations of some popular methods are summarized in the chart on the following page. For further information on these and other approaches to second-language instruction, refer to *Approaches and Methods in Language Teaching*, by Jack C. Richards and Theodore S. Rodgers, in the Cambridge Language Teaching Library.

Approach/Method	Advantages	Limitations
Grammar-translation Method (nineteenth–mid-twentieth centuries)	Explicit teaching of grammar rules; attention paid to language forms	Absence of communicative practice, which is an immediate need for new immigrants Reliance on translation, which is impractical in classes having students with many different first languages Focus on reading and translating texts; some adult students can't read in their first language
Direct Method (first part of twentieth century)	Grammar is taught Lessons begin with dialog or a story in the target language Use of visuals (actions, pictures, objects) to convey meaning	Inductive presentation is unsuitable for some adult students, who may benefit from overt explanations of rules Minimal reading and writing, which is needed by immigrant students with work or academic goals
Audiolingual Method (ALM) (1950s–1970s)	Emphasis on oral production Teacher models pronunciation Use of drills to reinforce grammatical patterns	Rote exercises reduce cognitive engagement Activities are designed to prevent learner errors, which reduces the need for students to negotiate meaning

Approach/Method	Advantages	Limitations
Cognitive Approach (1970s)	Grammar must be taught, either inductively or deductively	Emphasis on analyzing structure at the expense of communicative practice Pronunciation is de-emphasized
Natural Approach (1980s)	Language is presented in a "natural" sequence: listening, speaking, reading, writing Use of a communicative syllabus	Grammar is not overtly taught, yet many adult learners need and want grammar instruction Focus on input (listening) can delay output (speaking) that adults need immediately
Communicative Language Teaching (CLT) (1970s–today)	Communication is the goal of instruction Emphasis on meaningful interaction Course syllabus includes language functions Use of authentic texts and contexts	Focus on communication can result in ignoring grammar Emphasis on fluency at the expense of accuracy can result in many students never attaining correct grammar

Competency-based education (CBE)

CBE was adopted by many adult ESL programs in the late seventies to accommodate the large numbers of new refugees and immigrants who needed English immediately for survival and employment purposes (Parrish, 2004). It is still very popular today. Students learn language that will enable them to perform life-skills competencies, such as riding a bus, shopping at a supermarket, talking to a doctor, and so on. The instructional focus is on oral skills. Students are encouraged to speak from the very beginning, and communication is emphasized over grammatical accuracy.

The lack of attention paid to grammar in many CBE programs has turned out to be a drawback of the approach. Many former students from ESL programs with a CBE focus have poor reading and writing skills and little command of grammar even though they may be proficient speakers. Recently, many have returned to ESL classes in order to improve their English sufficiently to be able to help their children with schoolwork or to get a better job. Many adult ESL programs today maintain a curriculum based on competencies, but there is greater recognition of the need to concentrate on both grammatical accuracy and communication in ESL classes.

Larsen-Freeman's three-dimensional grammar model

We have established that adult ESL students need and want to learn grammar. However, in order for students to become truly competent users of English, it is not enough for us to present the form of the target structure. Unless we teach students how to apply or use the structure, we are not going far enough in helping them succeed.

Larsen-Freeman (2001) presents a model of grammar that goes beyond form. According to this framework, grammatical structures have three dimensions: form, meaning, and use. Let us take the modal *must* as an example:

Form	*must* + base form of verb (without *to*)
Meaning	obligation or necessity
Use	formal; used much more in writing than in speaking. In speaking, people tend to use *have to*.

If a student tells an American friend, "I must take my baby to the doctor," the friend will have no trouble understanding the student's meaning, but she might find the sentence strangely formal. Thus, Larsen-Freeman's framework has implications for the way we teach grammar. If students are unaware of all three dimensions of a grammatical structure, they may make mistakes even if they form the structure correctly.

Features of an eclectic approach to grammar instruction

Having reviewed the advantages and limitations of various language-teaching methods, what can we conclude about how we should approach grammar instruction in adult ESL courses? The most sensible approach appears to be an eclectic one that combines the most effective aspects of a variety of language-teaching methodologies. (See Richards and Rodgers, 2001, for their discussion of the "post-methods era.") Such an approach would include a focus on form with contextualized, communicative practice of the target structure. Additionally, such an eclectic approach would have the following characteristics:

- Students learn and practice grammar in a "natural" sequence: listening, speaking, reading, and writing.
- The teacher uses charts, actions, pictures, or objects to present the target grammar.
- Contexts for instruction come from everyday life.
- Classroom activities are interactive.
- Instruction includes attention to form, meaning, and use.
- Lessons include pronunciation practice.

The need to combine focus on form and communicative activities is evident from the lessons of CBE: Without a balance between grammar and communication, many students are not able to transition from ESL to higher education or to move up in their jobs. They remain stuck because of their inability to use correct grammar in all four skill areas – reading and writing as well as listening and speaking.

An eclectic approach is supported by many researchers who recognize that language instruction is context-dependent. In their chapter on the post-methods era, Richards and Rodgers (2001, 244–55) observe that "[c]hoice of teaching method cannot . . . be determined in isolation from other planning and implementation practices." Long (1991, cited in Nassaji and Fotos, 2004) proposes that the teacher draw students' attention to grammatical forms in the context of communication. This perspective is also advocated by Rodriguez (2009, 2), who says attention to form "should take place within a meaningful, communicative context, making it an extension of communicative language teaching, not a departure from it." Research has also shown that "teachers who focus students' attention on linguistic form during communicative interactions are more effective than those who never focus on form or who only do so in decontextualized grammar lessons" (Spada and Lightbown, 1993, and Lightbown, 1998, cited in Larsen-Freeman, 2001). Finally, there is evidence that students in programs that combine focus on form with communicative practice "show accelerated learning and substantial gains in usage ability compared to students in programs that provide only communicative exposure to target structures" (Azar, Folse, and Swan, 2009).

One challenge for curriculum developers and teachers is determining which forms to teach. Chapter 3 suggests ways to look at our learners and at characteristics of language to help make those decisions.

3 | Choosing Grammar to Teach

Adult immigrants and refugees have immediate needs to communicate in English – as parents, as members of the community, and as workers. In fact, federal legislation that authorizes funding for many adult ESL programs identifies this goal: "to provide learners with the language skills necessary to function in American society and to attain and retain a job" (Young and Morgan, 1994, cited in Rance-Roney, 1995). ESL programs that receive federal funds include community colleges, adult schools within an elementary and secondary system, and community-based organizations.

Adult immigrants and refugees also have limited time, which means that the language presented and practiced in the classroom must be immediately useful to students outside the classroom. One way of achieving such efficacy is by careful selection of grammar items to include in a curriculum.

With respect to the question of what grammar we choose to teach, this chapter addresses the following questions:

- Which factors determine the grammar that learners need?
- Which characteristics of language affect the selection of grammar?

Factors that determine the grammar learners need

Two important factors govern the selection of grammar in the adult ESL curriculum: (1) the language functions that students will need in their daily lives outside the classroom, and (2) the environment in which learners use English.

Functions needed in daily life. The term *function* refers to a speaker's purpose for communication. In turn, this communicative purpose can often be conveyed by specific grammatical structures, as shown in the chart below. For example, one way of describing one's past job duties (in a job interview, for instance) is to use the past tense. Thus a nursing assistant might answer the question, "What were your job duties?" with the statement, "I made beds and I helped patients."

Language function	Grammar structure
Describe past activities	Past tense *(made beds, helped patients)*
Request permission	Modals *can* or *may (Can I borrow your dictionary?)*
Give directions	Imperatives *(go straight, turn left)*

When selecting grammar to teach, we need to ask ourselves whether that grammar communicates a purpose that our learners truly need and whether, as a result, it is worth spending class time on a particular item. The subjunctive used for expressing urgency in sentences like *It's essential that he bring his passport* is an example of a structure that probably does not arise very often in the lives of our adult students, and as such might reasonably be omitted from our curriculum.

In short, English courses for adult immigrants should be designed around the communicative needs of the learners. The grammar we choose to include should closely match the functions that our students need in their daily lives.

The environment in which learners use English. The environment – where learners speak English and with whom they speak it – has important implications for the grammar we choose to teach.

First, in determining where learners use English, we need to look at four areas: the home, the community, the workplace, and the students' social milieu. Questions to consider with respect to learners' English use in these contexts include: Do our learners' children still use the home language, or is English now their language of choice? Do our learners live in communities in which their first language is dominant? Are their daily transactions, such as shopping and visits to the doctor, carried out in English? Do the students work in an English-speaking environment? Will they be using English in social situations?

The answers to these questions can help us determine the English that is most urgent for students to learn. If, for example, English is the preferred language of an adult learner's children, then the learner may need to use English in directing children to do household tasks. If, on the other hand, the children still use the home language, then the parents won't need English to perform this function. If learners shop for groceries in neighborhood stores where employees use their first language, then we may skip or postpone a unit on count and noncount food items. If learners are able to use their first language at work, they might not need to use English to report on work completed or to ask questions to clarify tasks; but if English is the dominant language at their workplace, then the functions of reporting and clarifying – and their associated grammar – are essential. Finally, if students will be using English in social situations, they will need "small talk," including functions such as describing plans *(I'm going to visit my grandmother)*, giving advice *(You should put your money in the bank)*, comparing interests *(I like dancing more than singing)*, and discussing health *(I've been coughing a lot recently)*.

The environment in which learners use English also includes the people that they will be speaking English with. In work situations, for example, will students be interacting with customers and supervisors, or only with co-workers? Will they need to use English to talk to their children's teachers, their children's friends, or the parents of their children's friends? The answers to these questions have an effect on the level of formality that students will need to master, and different levels of formality are associated with different grammatical structures. For example, a speaker may use a simple imperative when requesting something from a co-worker ("Get me a hammer."), whereas a more polite form ("Could you please get me a hammer?") is more appropriate in making a similar request of a supervisor.

When designing a grammar syllabus for a particular course or group of students, we need a way to identify the high-priority situations in which our learners will be using English and to whom they will be talking or writing. A needs assessment, such as a survey or a checklist, is a useful tool to identify these situations. The results can help us make choices regarding the grammar that is most needed by our learners.

Language characteristics that affect the selection of grammar

In determining whether or not to include a grammar item in a course syllabus, we need to look at the grammar from several different perspectives. These include the relationship between the grammar structure and the functions that the grammar expresses; how frequently the grammar is used; whether the grammar is essential for conveying meaning; how people actually use the grammar; and whether or not the grammar occurs in all four skill areas.

Relationship between grammatical structure and language function. As we have seen, we can often find a clear correlation between grammatical structure and language function. However, the same function may also be expressed by several different structures. For example, the function of giving advice can be conveyed in any of the following ways: (1) *You should study harder.* (2) *You had better study harder.* (3) *You ought to study harder.* (4) *You might study harder.* (5) *How about studying harder?* (6) *If I were you, I would study harder.*

Given that there are so many ways to give advice in English, how do we determine which structure(s) to teach at any given level? For lower-level learners, we could decide to teach just one structure – perhaps the form with *should*. With higher-level learners, we might choose to review the previously learned structures and add a new one; for example, a lesson targeting *ought to* might also review *should*. We can also target several structures in a lesson concerning the nuances between forms, such as the difference between *had better* and *should*. We might explain that *had better* is "stronger" and is therefore used in situations where a person with greater authority (such as a parent or supervisor) is speaking to a subordinate (i.e., a child or an employee). In contrast, *should*, which is not so strong, is proper to use with a wider range of people.

Such a lesson reinforces register (with whom and in what circumstances each structure is appropriate), an important concept for students to learn.

Some grammar items can also be used to express more than one function. An example is the modal *can*, which can denote the ability to do something *(I can type)*, asking permission *(Can I smoke here?)*, or granting permission *(I'm sorry your car is in the shop. You can drive my car.)*. To avoid overloading lower-level learners, in particular, we should not teach all these functions of *can* in the same lesson.

Frequency of use. When different structures can express the same language function, frequency of use is a second factor that may help us determine which structure(s) to teach and in what order. For example, future intention can be expressed by at least three different structures: *be going to* + verb *(I'm going to buy groceries this weekend)*, *will* + verb *(I think I'll go to a movie tonight)*, and the present continuous – *be* + verb + *-ing (I'm picking up my children after school)*. Corpus-based research shows that *be going to* is used most frequently to express this function, so most teachers would probably teach it first. At a higher level, we might teach *will* to describe future intention. We would probably not teach the third structure – the present continuous – until learners have learned to use it for its more common function, that is, to describe actions happening now.

Necessity for conveying meaning. Some grammatical forms, though correct, are not crucial to meaning. For example, the *-s* on third person singular verbs *(John lives, she studies, it costs)* is redundant because we are talking about only one person or thing as is made clear by a noun or pronoun. This does not mean we shouldn't teach the *-s* on third person singular verbs, but it does mean that we may spend less time on it than on other forms that are more critical to meaning, such as verb tenses.

Actual use. Grammar is dynamic; it changes over time. Changes tend to move the language toward greater regularity. An example is the distinction between *who* (subject case, as in *Who is she?*) and *whom* (object case, as in *Give it to whom?*). *Whom* is rarely heard in conversation anymore. Another example is *were* as used in the unreal conditional *(If I were married . . .)*. Over time, *if I were* has been regularized to *if I was*. Yet a third example is the distinction between adjectives and adverbs. For example, at one time, *slow* was used only as an adjective; now it often shows up in daily speech as an adverb *(We are coming to a school zone. Drive slow.)*.

As teachers, we need to be aware of how the language is changing and adjust our grammar syllabus to reflect those changes. We should avoid spending time on grammar that is not commonly used.

Occurrence in all four skill areas (listening, speaking, reading, and writing). Instruction in adult ESL programs usually follows the stages in which we acquire our first language: listening before speaking, speaking before reading, and reading before writing. Grammatical structures that are not common in spoken English do not lend themselves to adult ESL courses, which typically emphasize conversational situations. For example, the past perfect verb tense is seldom used in spoken English (Lane and Lange, 1999); rather, we use two simple past tenses. That is, *I ate before I went to the movie* is more common in spoken English than *I had eaten before I went to the movie*. Grammar structures that appear mainly in written English are best taught in higher-level classes that prepare students for higher education.

While most second-language educators nowadays agree that we need to teach grammatical form, the challenge lies in determining the most effective ways of focusing on form within a communicative approach. Chapters 4 through 6 provide an instructional framework for this eclectic approach.

4 The Grammar Lesson: Presentation

Up to now we have considered the role of grammar in adult ESL, and we have discussed the background and rationale for an eclectic teaching approach that combines a focus on form with communicative practice based on the functional needs of adult immigrant learners. The second half of the booklet concerns the grammar lesson itself. It addresses the instructional portion of the lesson, which is divided into three stages: presentation, guided practice, and communicative practice. Our primary focus will be on oral skills, since the need to speak fluently and accurately is a goal common to all of our adult immigrant learners.

In this chapter we take a close look at the presentation stage, in which the teacher introduces the target grammar in a meaningful context; explains the form, meaning, and use; and provides activities to check that students have understood what has been presented. The chapter addresses the following topics:

- An explicit versus implicit grammar presentation
- Learner variables affecting the selection of an explicit or implicit presentation
- The sequence of steps in a "hybrid" grammar presentation

Explicit or implicit presentation?

A teacher may choose to present new grammar either explicitly or implicitly. Broadly speaking, in an explicit presentation, the teacher begins by stating the grammar focus and explaining it, possibly using grammatical terms to do so. In contrast, when grammar is presented implicitly, the teacher may begin with an example that embeds the target grammar and may delay or avoid an overt explanation of the grammar.

Let's take a closer look at these two ways of presenting grammar.

Explicit presentation

In an explicit presentation, the teacher begins by announcing the grammar focus "Today we are going to learn about comparatives." We can write examples of the structure on the board or refer students to a grammar chart or box in the textbook. For example:

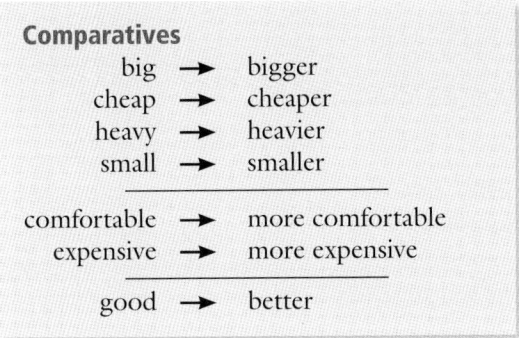

The teacher models the structure by reading the sentences on the board or in the textbook and then explains the form, meaning, and use (e.g., "The comparative means that two things are not the same. We use it to talk about the difference between two things.").

Alternatively, the teacher may choose not to explain anything about the target structure and may instead prefer to elicit this information from the students, especially if some of them are familiar with grammar terminology. For example, after the teacher writes sentences with the present continuous tense on the board and highlights the verb forms, the following exchange could take place:

Teacher: *How do we form the present continuous tense?*
Students: *Use* am, is, *or* are + *verb* -ing.
Teacher: *Is it happening now, or did it happen yesterday? What about tomorrow?*
Students: *Now, not yesterday and not tomorrow.*
Teacher: *What time words do we use with this tense?*
Students: *Now, right now, at this moment, today, this week.*

Implicit presentation

In an implicit grammar presentation, on the other hand, the teacher typically starts by saying the target structure in a meaningful context and avoiding analytical or technical explanations about the grammar. The presentation context may come from something in the classroom, from a visual such as a photo or an illustration in the textbook, or from the teacher's or students' own lives. The following examples illustrate these three contexts.

The classroom provides the context. In a lesson on the present continuous tense, the instructor might make sentences about things happening in the classroom:

I am teaching now. I am not eating.

José is listening to the teacher now. He is not writing.

José and Ana are listening to the teacher. They are not writing.

We are studying English now. We are not dancing.

Visuals provide the context. The teacher can point to a picture from the textbook or other source and form sentences using the target grammar. In a lesson on the modal *should*, students might view pictures of a house in disrepair and listen to the teacher make sentences about what the owners should do:

They should fix the roof.

They should plant flowers.

Recorded conversations accompanying illustrations in the textbook may provide additional opportunities for students to hear examples of the target grammar.

The teacher's and students' own lives provide the context. A unit on occupations might include a grammar lesson contrasting the present and past forms of the verb *to be*. The teacher could form model sentences such as the following:

I am an ESL teacher now. I was a piano teacher before.

My wife is a piano teacher now. She was an elementary school teacher before.

Daniel is a baker now. He was a hotel worker before.

Whether grammar is introduced explicitly or implicitly, the teacher should conclude the presentation stage by checking that students understand what has been taught. To check comprehension of the form of the present continuous, for instance, students might be asked to fill in the blanks in sentences like this: _____ *she* _____ *(work) now?* Or, to check that beginning students understand the difference between *is* and *was*, the teacher could show two pictures. The first, labeled *Before*, shows a woman dressed as a waitress; the other, labeled *Now*, shows the same woman as a nurse's assistant. The teacher makes statements like the following, and the students say, "yes" or "no."

> **Teacher:** *She is a waitress.* (No)
> **Teacher:** *She was a waitress.* (Yes)
> **Teacher:** *She was a nurse's assistant.* (No)
> **Teacher:** *She is a nurse's assistant.* (Yes)

Next, the teacher could point to the pictures and have the students make the statements, for example, "She is a nurse's assistant now. She was a waitress before."

Learner variables affecting an explicit or implicit presentation

A number of learner variables can help the teacher determine whether to present grammar explicitly or implicitly.

Language level. An explicit presentation, including an overt explanation of the target grammar and the use of grammatical terminology, is probably less effective with lower-level students who may not know enough English to be able to understand the explanation.

Educational background. Learners with limited education or literacy skills in their first language may not have a sense of the grammar of their own language or a command of grammatical terms (e.g., *verb tense*, *first person*, *pronoun*). With these learners, an implicit presentation may be more effective. On the other hand, students who have learned the grammar of their first language may respond well to an explicit explanation of grammar patterns and rules. Moreover, students who have studied English in their countries through a grammar-focused approach, such as grammar-translation, may believe that they are not learning English and may become impatient without a formal explanation of a new grammar pattern.

Goals for studying English. Students whose primary goal is survival in a new environment or finding and keeping an entry-level job need to be able to communicate, but they do not necessarily need to know grammar rules. An implicit presentation may suffice for these students. However, students with academic goals like passing the high-school equivalency test or going to community college, or those who have jobs requiring writing skills, need to learn grammar more explicitly than students with nonacademic goals. Ellis (1996) suggests that, in fact, "advanced speaking and writing proficiency, necessary for achievement of students' academic and vocational goals, may require explicit form-focused instruction."

A "hybrid" approach

As we know, adult ESL students have a wide range of backgrounds. Therefore, it may not be practical or desirable to employ a purely explicit or implicit approach when presenting grammar. A "hybrid" presentation that introduces the grammar implicitly, in a meaningful context, and also includes explicit explanation of form, meaning, and use, should probably be the rule of thumb in most cases.

The following chart shows what a prototypical hybrid presentation might look like. The left column, written as directions to the teacher, shows the steps in the presentation. The center column lists sample activities that could be used at each step. The right-hand column provides a chronological description of an actual lesson presentation on the past forms of *be* in the context of occupations.

Steps and activities in a "hybrid" grammar presentation
T = Teacher   Ss = Students

Step	Sample activities	Example
Provide examples of the target grammar in a meaningful context.	Use the target grammar in sentences based on: ■ what is happening in the classroom. ■ a visual. ■ the teacher's and/or students' own lives.	T draws a time line on the board with a past date (1979) on the left, the word *now* on the right, and several other dates in between. Below the year 1979 he writes *piano teacher*, and below the current date he writes *English teacher*. He then forms sentences about himself: *I am an English teacher now. I was a piano teacher before.* He writes the sentences on the board and underlines the verbs *am* and *was*. He provides a second example with sentences about his wife.
Check that Ss understand the meaning of the example(s).	■ Ask *Yes / No* questions. ■ Ask *or* questions. ■ Ask *Wh-* questions.	■ T underlines *is* and asks, "When?" Ss respond, "Now." T repeats with *was* and Ss respond, "Before." ■ T asks one S about his experience. (T: *Daniel, what is your job now?* Daniel: *Hotel worker.* T: *What was your job in Mexico?* Daniel: *Baker.* T to class: *Tell me about Daniel.* Class: *Daniel is a hotel worker now. He was a baker before.*)

Step	Sample activities	Example
Confirm that Ss understand meaning and use.	■ Ask questions that focus on when and/or why we use the target structure.	T points to various dates on the time line and asks, "Is that now or before?"
Provide an exercise or activity to check that Ss understand the form, meaning, and use of the target grammar.	■ Provide a series of sentences or a cloze passage in which students fill in the correct form. ■ Provide two choices, from which students select one.	T refers Ss to a fill-in-the-blank exercise in the book and has a volunteer do the first item. Ss finish the exercise on their own. T circulates to check understanding. When Ss have finished, volunteers put the answers on the board. T provides feedback.

5 The Grammar Lesson: Guided Practice

Once the teacher has presented the target grammar and checked that students understand the new structure's form, meaning, and use, the lesson moves on to the guided practice stage, "in which the learner manipulates the structure in question while all other variables are held constant" (Celce-Murcia and Hilles, 1988, 27). In this stage, learners make their first attempts at using the target grammar in meaningful – but controlled – contexts.

In guided practice activities, either the teacher or the textbook provides models for all the language that students will produce. Student responses are meaningful but not truly communicative, since there is usually only one or a limited choice of correct utterances. The overall goal of this stage is to help students build fluency with the target structure, that is, to begin using the structure without hesitancy or translation and with understandable pronunciation.

This chapter addresses the following topics in relation to guided practice:

- The importance of guided practice
- The teacher's role in guided practice
- Activities that provide guided practice
- Error correction in guided practice activities

The importance of guided practice

Guided practice provides a crucial bridge between the teacher's presentation of a new grammar structure and students' application of the new structure in communicative situations. By strictly controlling the context in which students use the target structure, we enable students to "gain control of the form without the added pressure and distraction of trying to use the form for communication" (Celce-Murcia and Hilles, 1988, 27). Most students need many opportunities for controlled practice of a new grammar pattern before they can use it communicatively.

The teacher's role in guided practice

Once the lesson moves into the practice stage, the teacher's main role is to guide or direct students in their first attempts to use the new structure in context. The following tasks and activities are included in this role:

Modeling the activity. The most common guided practice activities involve exchanges between students working in pairs. To build up students' readiness for the task, the teacher can lead the class through a progression consisting of (1) modeling both parts of the dialog; (2) having students listen and repeat; (3) taking one role and having students take the other; (4) dividing the class into two parts and having each group take one of the roles. Finally, students practice in pairs.

Checking that students understand the task. One way to check understanding is to have a student or students do the first item in an exercise. Another way is to have a student volunteer explain the task. Yet a third way is for the teacher to ask questions about the process ("Who listens and writes first, Student A or Student B? When Student B writes, what does Student A do?").

Monitoring. While students are working on their own, the teacher circulates to check that students are doing the task correctly and assists them as needed, including correcting individual students' errors in grammar and pronunciation. While monitoring, we may also collect examples of errors for follow-up exercises. Finally, we determine when students have had sufficient guided practice and are ready to move on to the next stage of the lesson.

Providing feedback. After the activity has concluded, the teacher should provide feedback on grammar and pronunciation errors that are common to all the students. Techniques for providing feedback are discussed in the section on error correction at the end of this chapter.

Activities that provide guided practice

Listening, speaking, reading, and writing can all be vehicles for guided practice activities. For example, drills and dialog substitutions involve listening and speaking. Conversation cards require reading as well as listening and speaking, and grids involve all four language skills. These and a selection of other popular activities are described in this section.

Drills can help adult learners commit grammar patterns to memory (Azar, Folse, and Swan, 2009). They also provide students with practice in pronouncing new patterns, helping them to become comfortable articulating the target language forms. Drills fall into two categories, mechanical and meaningful. Mechanical drills require minimal comprehension of content on the part of students and serve only to reinforce patterns. In a "backward buildup" drill, for instance, the teacher leads and students usually respond as a whole group.

> Teacher: *TV*
> Students: *TV*
> Teacher: *watching TV*
> Students: *watching TV*
> Teacher: *She is watching TV.*
> Students: *She is watching TV.*

In contrast, meaningful drills require students to understand the language in order to respond correctly, but the activity is tightly controlled because only one answer is possible. The following is an example of a "substitution" drill focusing on pronouns:

> Teacher: (holding up a picture of a woman watching TV) *What is she doing?*
> Students: *She is watching TV.*
> Teacher: (holding up a picture of a man eating dinner) *What is he doing?*
> Students: *He is eating dinner.*

Dialog substitutions are short conversations (usually two to four exchanges) that students repeat, each time substituting different vocabulary but repeating the target grammar. In the following example, focusing on the future with *be going to*, students look at pictures of people dressed to do different activities. They read and practice the model. Then, working in pairs, they repeat the conversation, replacing the boldface words with the numbered cues.

> **Student 1:** *What's **Brian** going to do today?*
> **Student 2:** *He's going to **go to the beach**.*
> **Student 1:** *That sounds like fun.*
>
> 1. Brian / go to the beach
> 2. Ali / go shopping
> 3. Lisa / play soccer
> 4. Hiro and Lee / go fishing
> 5. Andrea / take a trip
> 6. Ray / go to a birthday party

An advantage of dialog substitutions is that students are practicing actual conversations that may be applicable to their daily lives.

Grids (also called charts) present information for students to use in forming questions and answers. Grids differ from dialog substitutions in that the cues for speaking require reading rather than recognition of pictures. For example, the following grid is designed for practicing *Yes / No* questions, short answers, and long answers with the present tense of *have*.

	Headache	Backache	Toothache
Tom	Yes	No	No
Mary	No	No	Yes
(you)			

Using the cues in the grid, students conduct conversations like the following:

> **Student 1:** *Does Tom have a headache?*
> **Student 2:** *Yes, he does. He has a headache.*

As shown, grids often include a place for students to answer with their own information – the "you" row in the grid. This pushes the exercise to a slightly more communicative level.

At higher levels, grids may have significantly more print, as in this guided exercise for practicing real and unreal conditionals:

Real	Unreal
Stay home / Have a party with his friends	Travel to Florida / Spend New Year's Eve near the beach
Go to his parents' house / Have a quiet celebration with his family	Be in Mexico / Eat 12 grapes at midnight

Using the cues, students produce sentences like these:

If Victor stays home on New Year's Eve, he will have a party with his friends.

If Victor traveled to Florida, he would spend New Year's Eve near the beach.

Conversation cards are index cards (or strips of paper) that provide cues for guided conversations between two students. For example, cards like these can be used to practice verb tenses:

The Grammar Lesson: Guided Practice

play cards	watch TV	study

Each student receives a card. Students stand up and move around the room, pairing up with any classmate they meet. Student 1 asks a question, which remains constant; Student 2 answers according to the information on his or her card. The students then switch roles, as in this example targeting the future tense with *be going to*:

> **Student 1:** *What are you going to do this evening?*
> **Student 2:** *I'm going to watch TV. What are you going to do this evening?*
> **Student 1:** *I'm going to play cards.*

After both students have practiced the question and the answer, they exchange cards and each moves on to talk to a different classmate.

In addition to reinforcing the target grammar, conversations based on conversation cards expose students to a wide range of vocabulary items. Students also enjoy the opportunity to interact with a variety of classmates.

Word strips are sentences cut up into words. Students arrange the words to form questions or statements. These two examples provide practice with the present perfect tense.

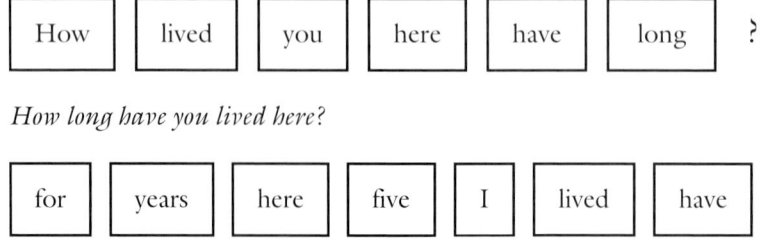

How long have you lived here?

I have lived here for five years.

Word strips are especially effective with kinesthetic learners – students who learn best by moving or manipulating objects. The strips also reinforce the connection between spoken and written English.

Find someone who. In this interview activity, students have a two-column grid with cues in the left column. They circulate and ask questions based on the cues. When a classmate answers "Yes" to a question, students write that person's name in the right-hand column. In the following example, students are using the simple past tense to talk about their previous evening's activities:

> **Student 1:** *Ricardo, did you cook dinner last night?*
> **Ricardo:** *No, I didn't.*
> **Student 1:** *Anna, did you cook dinner last night?*
> **Anna:** *Yes, I did.*
> **Student 1:** *Robby, did you empty the trash last night?*
> **Robby:** *Yes, I did.*

Find someone who . . .	Classmate's name
cooked dinner last night	Anna
emptied the trash yesterday	Robby

The language on the grid is sometimes different from the form that students will use to ask the question. In the example, students need to remember to drop the *-ed* from the verb and to begin questions with *Did* (e.g., "Did you cook dinner last night?").

Information transfer activities require students to take information presented in one form and put it into another form. For example, in an activity designed for practicing prepositions of location (*next to, across from, between*, etc.), students are given both a short narrative reading that describes the locations of places in a neighborhood and a map of the neighborhood with the names of the locations omitted. Using the information from the reading, students write the names of the places in the appropriate locations on the map.

Information gap activities usually consist of two worksheets labeled A and B. They contain some information that is the same, but each worksheet is also missing some information that is found on the other sheet. Partners must ask each other questions in order to get the information missing from their respective sheets. In this example, students practice asking and answering personal information questions using the possessive adjectives *his* and *her*. The first item in each student's worksheet is filled in as an example.

> **Student 1:** *What's his first name?*   **Student 2:** *What's her first name?*
> **Student 2:** *His first name is Adam.*   **Student 1:** *Her first name is Maria.*

Student 1

First name:	Adam	First name:	Maria
Last name:	Chang	Last name:	
Middle name:		Middle name:	Elena
Zip code:	10034	Zip code:	
Area code:		Area code:	212
Phone number:	555-3158	Phone number:	

Student 2

First name:	Adam	First name:	Maria
Last name:	Chang	Last name:	Mora
Middle name:	Edward	Middle name:	
Zip code:		Zip code:	95667
Area code:	212	Area code:	
Phone number:		Phone number:	555-9072

Though guided, information gap activities mirror real-life interactions in that listeners do not know the missing information until their partners supply it.

Error correction in guided practice activities

Error correction may be either overt or indirect; the choice depends on a number of variables.

Overt versus indirect correction. In overt error correction, the teacher corrects by providing the correct form. We may decide to repeat only the part of the sentence containing the error and then provide the correct form, as follows:

> **Student:** *I go to school yesterday.*
> **Teacher:** *Not* go, went.

Or we can repeat the entire sentence correctly and point out the student's error, saying, for instance, "I went to school yesterday, not I go to school yesterday." Overt correction is usually followed by having the student repeat the sentence with the correct form.

An indirect correction technique involves cuing students in the hope that they will be able to correct the error by themselves. If this attempt is unsuccessful, however, the correction may need to be more overt, as the following example demonstrates:

> **Student:** *I go to school yesterday.*
> **Teacher:** *Is yesterday present or past?*
> **Student:** *Past.*
> **Teacher:** *Try the sentence again.*
> **Student:** *I go to school yesterday.*
> **Teacher:** *You went to school when?*
> **Student:** *Yesterday.*
> **Teacher:** *Go or went?*
> **Student:** *Went.*

We can also cue students without using grammatical terms, as in this next example:

> **Student:** *I go to school yesterday.*
> **Teacher:** *You went to school when?*
> **Student:** *Yesterday.*
> **Teacher:** *Go or went?*
> **Student:** *Went.*

Using cues encourages students to stop and think rather than just repeating what the teacher says. This technique requires students to apply what they "know" but are not yet able to use correctly. An argument in support of this technique is that it may help students learn to correct themselves outside the classroom as well.

The choice of an overt versus an indirect correction technique depends on the nature of both the activity and the learner. When students are engaged in mechanical practice designed to reinforce patterns, such as drills, we may prefer to correct errors overtly, especially if students are responding as a whole class or as a group. When correcting individual students, we need to consider the background and confidence of the learner in determining whether to correct errors overtly. Learners with a limited educational background or limited literacy skills in their first language may lack self-confidence in learning English; for them, error correction may be frustrating and may lower their self-confidence even more. On the other hand, learners who have studied grammar before or who plan to attend college may be frustrated if their errors aren't corrected, as they may believe that language learning equals the study of grammar.

Follow-up error correction exercises. As stated at the beginning of this chapter, one of the teacher's tasks during the guided practice stage is to circulate and take note of errors that students make while they are practicing. There are various techniques for providing feedback on the errors we have collected. One way is to put the errors on the board and invite volunteers to come up and correct them. Alternatively, corrections may be elicited from the whole class. Another technique is for the teacher to create a worksheet based on students' errors. For errors in pronunciation (important in some areas of grammar, as with the past tense *-ed* marker, which has three different pronunciations depending on the sound immediately before it), the teacher might provide listen-and-repeat drills to reinforce the correct pattern.

The advantage of going over errors collectively at the end of the guided activity is that this technique focuses students' attention on the errors, not on the students who made them.

6 The Grammar Lesson: Communicative Practice

As we have seen, each stage of the grammar lesson has a specific purpose and specific steps. At the presentation stage, the teacher introduces and explains the target grammar and then checks that students understand the new structure's form, meaning, and use. At the guided practice stage, students manipulate the target grammar in controlled contexts, using models provided by the teacher or materials, but they do not have to generate new language. At last, in the communicative stage, learners have the opportunity to use the target grammar as they listen, speak, read, and write about real, meaningful topics in their lives. As in the guided stage, many activities are conducted in pairs, in small groups, or with the whole class; however, language use at this stage is less controlled and more spontaneous than in the previous one. In fact, most communicative activities involve much more language than just the target grammar. For example, a discussion about ways to avoid catching the flu could be designed to practice modals of advice (*should, shouldn't, had better*, etc.) and might naturally also involve students sharing their experiences of having the flu, getting a flu vaccine, and so on.

As in Chapter 5, the main emphasis of this chapter is on interactive activities for listening and speaking practice. However, suggestions for follow-up activities involving reading and writing are also provided. This chapter addresses the following topics:

- The importance of communicative practice
- The teacher's role in communicative practice activities
- Communicative activities that reinforce grammar
- Error correction in communicative activities

The importance of communicative practice

Communicative practice is important because it reflects real language use outside the classroom. In the real world, we determine what we say but have no control over what we hear in response. When meaning isn't clear, we negotiate and adjust our language so that we can understand or be understood by others. Take, for example, the following exchange:

> **Student 1:** *What do you think of the weather?*
> **Student 2:** *It's too hot today!*
> **Student 1:** *But I thought you like warm weather. Do you mean "too hot" or "very hot"?*
> **Student 2:** *Oh, sorry. I mean it's very hot. Just the way I like it!*

Well-designed communicative activities provide a need for students to understand each other. They create an opportunity for students to hone their negotiation skills in the safety of the classroom. Through a listener's response to them, students discover how well they are using the target grammar. If they use the grammar incorrectly and a misunderstanding occurs, they learn to adjust their language in order to communicate.

The teacher's role in communicative practice activities

The communicative phase of the grammar lesson is highly student-centered. The teacher acts mainly as a facilitator or manager, performing the following tasks.

Modeling the activity. At this stage, our main concern is modeling the task rather than the language students will produce. To be sure students understand the task, we can read the directions and then ask questions to check that students know what to do. We may also demonstrate the activity with a student or have two students demonstrate it before dividing the class into pairs or groups to work independently.

Setting up the grouping. Whether an activity involves partners or small groups, students should know with whom they will be working. If students choose their own partner or form their own group, the teacher should confirm that everyone has a partner or a group. If the activity involves mingling, we may need to encourage reluctant students to get up and move around.

Providing a process for students to report back. This step is essential in communicative practice because it builds in individual accountability. When students know they will be reporting back on the task, they are less apt to digress. Mechanisms for reporting back include grids for individual notetaking, written summaries, or having one student in a group report on the group's work at the end of the activity.

Monitoring. As with guided practice, the teacher circulates while students are doing the activity but largely avoids interrupting to help as that can eliminate the need for students to negotiate and adjust their language when there is a misunderstanding. The main purpose of monitoring at the communicative stage is to identify problems students encounter as they do the activity in order to determine the need for follow-up error-correction activities.

Providing feedback. As a rule, feedback for communicative activities is provided to the whole class after the activity has concluded. At this stage, the teacher has the same options as with guided practice (e.g., writing errors on the board or creating a worksheet based on observed errors). If, while monitoring, we notice that students lack strategies for negotiating and adjusting their language, we may model a specific strategy, such as asking for clarification or repetition (e.g., *Did you say . . . ?*), and provide an activity for students to practice that strategy. We might also tell the class about successful negotiation strategies that individual students employed during the activity. Praising students for their work is also appropriate at this time.

Communicative activities that reinforce grammar

Many communicative activities are similar to those described in Chapter 5. Again, the difference between the guided and communicative versions of activities is that in communicative practice, interactions may include more content than just the target grammar, and students are freer to choose the context of their utterances.

Interview grids. In this activity, students work in small groups or walk around and mingle, asking and answering questions. They take notes on their classmates' answers in a chart. In the following example, students use *because* and *because of* to talk about their lives in the United States.

Student 1: Shakir, why did you come to this country?
Student 2: I came because of my children. I wanted to be near them.
Student 1: Why do you live in this neighborhood?
Student 2: Because it is close to my job.

Name	Why did you come to this country?	Why do you live in this neighborhood?
Shakir	Children live here	Close to his job

To conclude the activity, the teacher can replicate the chart on the board and fill it in based on students' reporting on those they interviewed. Students may also be asked to use the information in the chart to write sentences or paragraphs about their classmates.

Conversation cards. In this activity, presented earlier in Chapter 5, students ask and answer each other's questions, then exchange cards and move on to talk to a different student. In the guided version, all students ask the same question; they answer based on cues written on the cards. In the communicative version, the cards contain cues to the questions and the answers come from the students. For example, these conversation cards can be used to practice the present perfect tense:

What is a food in the United States you haven't tried yet?	Have you begun to read a book in English yet?	What is a household chore you've already done this week?

As a follow-up, students can make sentences about someone they interviewed (e.g., *Asha hasn't tried fried chicken yet. José hasn't begun to read a book in English yet. Esperanza has already done the laundry this week.*).

Opinion sharing. One of the simplest yet most enjoyable communicative activities involves students sitting in pairs or small groups and comparing values, opinions, or beliefs. Such discussions often have the added benefit of helping to develop skills other than grammar, such as turn-taking, agreeing or disagreeing, and of course negotiating meaning if a misunderstanding occurs. In the following example, students practice using superlative adjectives:

Ask and answer questions about your community. Use the cues. Add your own questions.

1. clothing store – biggest
2. clothing store – lowest prices
3. supermarket – cheapest
4. restaurant – best
5. ??

To bring closure to this activity, the teacher might have each small group share its answers. We can also record students' answers in a grid on the board, then ask the class to draw conclusions regarding the information (e.g., "What do you think is the biggest clothing store in our community?"). As with other communicative activities, we can also ask students to follow the speaking activity with writing.

Jigsaw. In this activity, different students have different pieces of information, which they must share in order to make a whole. Students typically work in groups of three or four. Each student receives a strip of paper with his or her piece of information. Students take turns speaking and listening. In the example that follows, each student has read about a different employee being considered for Employee of the Year. They use the present perfect tense to share their information and then select the best candidate.

> **A.** There are four different candidates for Employee of the Year. Each person in your group has information about a different candidate. Read your paragraph. Then talk with others in your group. Ask and answer the questions to complete the chart.
>
> | Questions | Candidates | | | |
> |---|---|---|---|---|
> | | 1 | 2 | 3 | 4 |
> | How many times has . . . been absent? | | | | |
> | How long has . . . worked for the company? | | | | |
> | How productive has . . . been? | | | | |
> | What has . . . done to deserve a promotion? | | | | |
>
> **B.** After you have completed the chart, discuss which of the four candidates should be Employee of the Year. Be prepared to share the reasons for your decision.

Often, to ensure that students are ready to share with classmates whose pieces of information are different, the teacher first has students work with others who have the same information.

After students have completed their discussion, we can bring the whole class together and have each group share its decision and the reasons for its choice (e.g., "We think candidate number 3 should be Employee of the Year for several reasons. He has never been absent. He has worked for the company since 1995. We think he has been the most productive of all the candidates because . . . He has done several things to deserve the award. For example, he . . ."). We can follow up by asking students to write a paragraph for the company newsletter about the new Employee of the Year.

Problem solving. Students are presented with a problem or set of problems, either orally or in writing. They discuss the problem(s), identifying issues and suggesting possible solutions. To conclude the activity, students share their suggestions, and the teacher writes them on the board. The class can then vote on the best solution.

In this example, students discuss people's money problems using the modals *could* (for suggestions) and *should* (for advice).

Work in a small group. Make suggestions or give advice.

1. Helen spends too much money on food.

    She could use coupons.

    She could shop at discount stores.

    She could buy in bulk.

    She could stop eating out.

    I think she should make a budget for food.

2. Gregory spends too much money on clothes.
3. Teresa spends too much money on rent.
4. Yousef spends too much money on cell phone calls.

Role play. Students are given information that places them in an imaginary situation. They then act out the situation in pairs or groups. The following role play provides practice with the past tense.

Student 1

You are a police officer responding to a 911 call about a burglary. Ask questions to get information about the crime. For example:
What time did you go to sleep last night?
Did you hear any strange noises during the night?
What did the burglar take?
How did the burglar get in?
??

Student 2

You woke up this morning and discovered that during the night, someone entered your home through the bathroom window. The burglar took all your money, your jewelry, and your passport. You didn't wake up during the night, and you didn't hear anything.

You called 911 and a police officer came to your home. Answer the officer's questions.

There are many ways to follow up on a role play. One option is to have volunteers repeat their role play for the class. Another is to have students write a paragraph about the incident in the role play.

In addition to providing practice with grammar, role plays give students an opportunity to practice communicating in new social contexts and in different registers (e.g., to colleagues such as classmates, fellow tenants, or co-workers versus to "superiors" such as teachers, landlords, or employers).

Error correction in communicative activities

At the communicative stage, students are participating in genuine exchanges of information. They become very involved as they talk and learn from one another. For this reason, teachers should not interrupt students to correct errors unless communication between them breaks down completely. It is preferable for us to take notes on significant errors and go over them with the whole class once the activity has finished.

Conclusion

A challenge for teachers in ESL classes for adult learners is to deliver lessons that are effective when students within any one class fall along a continuum, ranging from students who have no formal education and cannot read or write in their first language, to students who may have a postgraduate degree and have studied several languages. Grammar lessons are especially challenging, since some students may have little knowledge of the grammar of their first language, and others not only understand the grammar of their first language but believe that learning grammar is all that is needed to learn a language.

Teachers, too, fall along a continuum – ranging from those who emphasize grammar over communication in their teaching to those who stress communication with little focus on form. Perhaps this booklet will persuade teachers with a heavy communicative orientation to incorporate more focus on form into their teaching; conversely, teachers with a heavy grammar orientation may be convinced of the value of presenting grammar within a communicative framework based on functions and situations that adult ESL students face in their everyday lives.

This booklet should also help teachers evaluate instructional materials. To determine the appropriateness of materials for our adult students, we can ask questions such as the following:

- Do the materials present the grammar in contexts that are meaningful for our students?

- Do grammar explanations include information not only on form but also meaning and use?

- Do students hear the grammar before they are expected to produce it? Do they read it before being asked to write it?

- Are there visuals?

- Do the materials provide opportunities for students to produce the target grammar in speaking and writing tasks that they might encounter outside the classroom?

- Is there a clear and logical progression from presentation to guided practice to communicative practice?

Finally, we need to remind ourselves that with low-level students, implicit presentations of grammar will be more effective than explicit, but because we also have more sophisticated students, we must incorporate explicit presentations as well. As Rodriguez (2009, 4) concludes, "To help learners improve their grammatical accuracy, instructors should embed explicit focus on form within the context of meaningful learning activities and tasks that give learners ample opportunities for practice."

References

Azar, B., Folse, K., and Swan, M. (2009). "Teaching Grammar in Today's Classroom." Panel discussion, TESOL 2008. Available online at www.azargrammar.com.

Bitterlin, G., Johnson, D., Price, D., Ramirez, S., and Savage, K. L. (2008). *Ventures*. New York: Cambridge University Press.

Bitterlin, G., Johnson, D., Price, D., Ramirez, S., and Savage, K. L. (2009). *Ventures Professional Development DVD*. New York: Cambridge University Press.

Celce-Murcia, M. (Ed.). (2001). *Teaching English as a Second or Foreign Language, Third Edition*. Boston: Heinle & Heinle.

Celce-Murcia, M., and Hilles, S. (1988). *Techniques and Resources in Teaching Grammar*. New York: Oxford University Press.

Ellis, R. (1996). "SLA and Language Pedagogy." In A. Rodriguez (Ed.), *Teaching Grammar to Adult English Language Learners: Focus on Form*. Washington, DC: Center for Applied Linguistics.

Ellis, R. (2001). "Investigating Form-Focused Instruction." In A. Rodriguez (Ed.), *Teaching Grammar to Adult English Language Learners: Focus on Form*. Washington, DC: Center for Applied Linguistics.

Fotos, S. (2001). "Cognitive Approaches to Grammar Instruction." In M. Celce-Murcia (Ed.), *Teaching English as a Second or Foreign Language, Third Edition*. Boston: Heinle & Heinle.

Hilles, S., and Sutton, A. (2001). "Teaching Adults." In M. Celce-Murcia (Ed.), *Teaching English as a Second or Foreign Language, Third Edition*. Boston: Heinle & Heinle.

Jones, L. (2007). *The Student-Centered Classroom*. New York: Cambridge University Press.

Lane, J., and Lange, E. (1999). *Writing Clearly*. Boston: Heinle & Heinle.

Larsen-Freeman, D. (2001). "Teaching Grammar." In M. Celce-Murcia (Ed.), *Teaching English as a Second or Foreign Language, Third Edition*. Boston: Heinle & Heinle.

Nassaji, H., and Fotos, S. (2004). "Current Developments in Research on the Teaching of Grammar." *Annual Review of Applied Linguistics, 24*, 126–45.

Parrish, B. (2004). *Teaching Adult ESL.* New York: McGraw-Hill.

Parrish, B. (May 2009). "Where's the Grammar in Competency-Based Instruction?" *AEIS Newsletter,* 7(1).

Rance-Roney, J. (1995). "Transitioning Adult ESL Learners to Academic Programs." *ERIC Digest ED385173.*

Richards, J. (2006). *Communicative Language Teaching Today.* New York: Cambridge University Press.

Richards, J., and Rodgers, T. (2001). *Approaches and Methods in Language Teaching.* New York: Cambridge University Press.

Rodriguez, A. (2009). "Teaching Grammar to Adult English Language Learners: Focus on Form." *CAELA Network Brief.* www.cal.org/caelanetwork/pdfs/TeachingGrammarFinalWeb.pdf